It's a Slower Waltz

To La Zuita

Harriette Lanigo-Ludich

Oct. 11, 2005

*I*n just six months I will celebrate my 90th birthday. This auspicious observance amazes me because I am publishing a second book. I feel it is a valediction of my ability to leave behind something to show for all the years I have been putting words together.

My newspaper experience goes back to the 1920s when my father, a country newspaperman in Nebraska, allowed me to print my first column.

Most of these selected essays have appeared in the *Bennington* (Vt.) *Banner.* Others have been chosen from an accumulation of articles written at other times in my life.

My first publishing effort was an incentive to do it all over again. If you have read *Awful Green Stuff and the Nakedness of Trees*, you may want to turn the pages of *It's a Slower Waltz.*

— Harriette Lerrigo-Leidich
Fall 2001

It's a Slower Waltz

Memorable Days from a Long Life

A BEECH SEAL PRESS BOOK
published by
IMAGES FROM THE PAST
BENNINGTON, VERMONT

Cover: Detail from "Riverscape, Westport, Massachusetts 1985" in watercolor and pastel by Mary E. Natalizia (whitman@bcn.net)

1 2 3 4 5 6 7 8 9 10 XXX 10 09 08 07 06 05 04 03 02 01

Library of Congress Cataloging-in-Publication Data

CIP applied for

Copyright© 2002 Harriette Lerrigo-Leidich
Published by Images from the Past, Inc.
P.O. Box 137, Bennington, VT 05201
Tordis Ilg Isselhardt, Publisher

Printed in the United States of America

Design and Production: Susan Mathews/Stillwater Studio, Stillwater, NY
Printer: Thomson-Shore, Inc., Dexter, MI
Text: Adobe Garamond   *Display:* Fairfield
Paper: 60lb. Writers Offset B21 Natural
Cover: 12pt. C1S

Contents

It's a Slower Waltz

*T*oday as I reached down to put on my hose I suddenly noticed that toes that were once straight were beginning to point NNE and NNW on the same foot. Horrors! I noticed changes in hands and wrists, too and know that this process happens as one grows older.

Seems that in the morning the beverage cup gets a bit heavier. It is not unusual to spill the orange juice, overpour the cereal, jiggle the cream pitcher and spill the sugar. To get up from the table is not as easy as in the past. The old bones grow less agile.

But I'm learning patience. No rushing to start the day which now begins with a cup of Postum instead of coffee. And there is that slowing gait with the household chores. It is important not to be rushed.

There are some nice things happening too as I age. Growing older means taking my ease with every task. Truly life is not dull and monotonous if you take time to grow old gracefully.

I like to play cards. It is good exercise although it takes some doing to shuffle cards with arthritic fingers. Furthermore it is a good sharpener of your mental faculties. When I have to ask someone what game I'm playing then I will know that I am truly old.

I'm trying to not let the world pass me by as I count the years past the Biblical three score and ten. The spots on the hands do not dismay me too much as I know they are a badge of age, not a scourge. Crows' feet are not age lines to me — they are laugh lines. The once supple limbs are on the flabby side. I'm too old for aerobics now.

In another town where I lived I did join a "Nifty Fifties" slimnastics group. Honestly I felt more like a "Slower Seventy" person but those sessions taught me something about constantly exercising.

It has helped me to think old positively by visiting others my age. I often come away from those visits with much sadness. I see deterioration of mind and body negativism and despair. It makes me realize how fortunate I am to be hale and hearty, despite my half-hearted complaints. I'm not ready for a retirement home just yet.

I'm trying to care for my body and mind in a simple objective way. I cook and eat the right nutritious food. It always pains me to see an older person in the supermarket with a cart loaded with pastries, ice cream, snacks, TV dinners and candy.

Life is an eventful and interesting and challenging journey from infancy, childhood, youth, marriage and offspring. You watch your children grow up with all their adventures and misadventures. Then comes the half century mark and those golden years are soon to follow. There is that ultimate recognition that we are all mortal facing a process called aging. Life for me now is a slower dance, but I'm still waltzing and enjoying every step.

Class in the Old Days

When I saw the picture in Vermont's *Bennington Banner* of teachers unpacking books and supplies at Catamount Elementary School, I wondered if that same new book smell emanates from the books as it did when I went to school. Back in Iowa where I went to school (and where I was born) we had to buy books, notebooks, pencils and tablets. I liked the smell of new books and believed it was an inky smell that lingered long after we began using them. Sometimes we did not have the luxury of new books and in our family we had hand-me-downs or used books. The curriculum didn't change much in those days.

When we moved to Nebraska, school books were furnished but not paper supplies. While a bit incapacitated recently I thought about the small school I attended. Two grades were in one room with the same teacher. It was possible to hold some classes together and one of them we shared was art. What a miserable failure I was at that! The school had a hectograph that was a machine using a glycerin-coated layer of gelatin to duplicate copies. That is how the outline of birds, flowers and art pictures were presented to us.

Our assignment was to color the birds and flowers with water color paints. These were in a long slim tin box and usually contained only the primary colors; we learned to make other colors by mixing to give us the right hue. My robins didn't really have the right colored red-brown breast nor did the bluebirds seem to be the blue they were naturally. After art classes the pictures were hung around the slate blackboard; mine never seemed to sparkle!

Paper was sparingly distributed. Today, workbooks, notebooks and library books are furnished by the school system. Even our pencils had a hard lead which made them last longer. The erasers were always worn down to the edge as that is how we corrected our work.

When we used pen and ink for our Palmer Method writing the ink was furnished by the school and poured into an inkwell at the right hand corner of our desks from a large bottle. We had to furnish our own cork holder for pen nibs. A grooved slot in the desks held our single pencil.

Recess was always looked forward to and we would go flying out of the classroom to claim the swings, teeter-totter or merry-go-round. We had a morning and afternoon recess and I remember there was always a teacher standing around to see that no altercations took place.

Town children went home for lunch. No hot lunch then and only pupils who came from the country brought their lunch pails. I still remember that old bread and apple smell that permeated the cloakroom where they stashed their tin lunch pails.

I can name the teachers I had from the first to sixth grades. Of course the dearest one was the first-grade teacher, Miss Canty. She became my first mother-away-from-home. Instead of the casual clothes like the teachers wear today, Miss Canty wore a long black skirt and a white blouse with a high neck and always a brooch of some kind. I rather liked the authority that she portrayed because of her stylized mode of dress.

We were in the classroom almost eight hours a day and did our lessons in planned study periods. No books to carry home in a big heavy book bag like they carry today. How different schools are now. Lots of paper, art supplies, library books, physical education, graphic materials and of course the ubiquitous computer. I don't know if children will be happy when school "takes up" in a week or so, but I was always glad to hear the school bell (and we did have a school bell that rang out) call us back to the little rooms where we learned the 3 Rs. Back then there is something we didn't have that is so common today — home work!

About Hollyhocks and African Violets

As I looked over my few African violets I'm trying to cultivate it made me think about house plants my mother used to bring indoors after a summer outside. Nothing fancy like African violets back then, but begonias, geraniums, sansevieria, Christmas cacti and maybe a spiky aloe. Those plants given a taste of summer added new growth. Then came the time to bring them indoors as frost time neared.

Most housewives back then filled a southern exposure window with their house plants. Sometimes an enterprising husband made a tier of shelves and the plants were arranged and rearranged according to need for light. I'm not sure there were any of the many plant foods such as we have now; just a good healthy green thumb kept the plants coming along indoors.

I wanted to grow some outside flowers after I moved to Vermont. My first choice was the old-fashioned hollyhocks which are native to China. My neighbor had a huge bed of them and gave me some seed. These I expectantly planted indoors for transplanting later outside.

My daughter-in-law with the green thumb transplanted the fragile plants and I offered up a prayer that they would root and bring forth much-looked for blooms. The first year the plants grew about 18 inches and looked healthy. They are a biennial plant so I didn't expect blooms that year. I could wait! But this year what a gratification to see that my hollyhocks grew to over five feet and put out various colored blooms. They occupy a small part of a little garden area I have staked out and I glory in their beauty.

In the little Kansas town where we used to live my old neighbor had a whole backyard of hollyhocks and my young son thought they were the most beautiful flower. I treasure a Brownie box camera shot of him on his tricycle in front of those hollyhocks.

I'm enjoying my small patch of hollyhocks because I know that next year they won't bloom. I believe they will spread and some day I may have quite a showy patch of them.

But back to the African violets. I have some that bloom at various times, two of which are always vying for blooming honors. There is one reluctant plant that sits on the side of the window sill just taking up space. I'm hoping that some day it will surprise me — and itself — and send forth a lovely bloom which will match or exceed the beauty of my other plants.

Autumnal Memories

*W*ith some leaves beginning to turn in our area, other weather changes are going on in other parts of the country. I'm thinking particularly of how things are back in Iowa and Nebraska when fall comes around and they begin to think about husking the corn. Iowa has been known as the state "where the tall corn grows," and Kansas, where I also lived, grew corn as well as wheat.

One of the Kansas farmers was so proud of his tall corn that he brought us a stalk 16 feet tall and we placed it at the entrance of our newspaper office. Then we posed in front of it with the printer's devil and our little country gal who gathered local news. That tall cornstalk evoked a lot of comment.

As a youngster I noted that corn was planted in check-rows. That is you could look down the rows from any angle and they would all be straight. Corn was planted with listers and the seeds fell in a symmetrical pattern. Farmers used to say that by June the corn was knee high and then by July 4 they counted on having roasting ears along with new peas grown in the family garden.

When I moved to the Cornhusker state of Nebraska I learned how cornhusking was done. The huskers would wear a glove that had a hook on it to snap off the ears, and throw them against the bangboard of the wagon that a team pulled up and down the field. There were times when good deeds were done for farmers unable to do all their own ingathering, and there would be several wagons in the corn fields.

After the corn was husked a cutter would come in and chop up the stalks for ensilage and it would be placed in the silo. They never wasted anything back in those days.

Corn was shelled and hauled to the elevators in town. Every town had a grain elevator which accepted the corn and it was loaded into box cars and sent off by rail to manufacturing plants. Likewise wheat was also trucked to the elevators to be blown into box cars for shipment.

The little town where I lived when I first married had a busy elevator and I liked to go there in in the fall just to watch the operations. There was a certain smell to the grain, particularly the wheat and I even tasted a few grains. I knew that grain in those box cars would end up in some cereal or flour product.

I went back to that little town in Kansas last fall and to my dismay there was no elevator. Everything is shipped by truck now; no more of those tall buildings with shafts to shunt the grain into boxcars. In fact, the railroad tracks were even ripped up.

My, how things have changed. Over the past 60 years many changes have occurred in the way farm products are grown and marketed. We don't see check-rows of corn, but hybrid varieties all the same height and harvested with modern equipment. No spring wagons on which you could add another sideboard so you could haul more ears of corn. As a matter of fact I don't really know how they do all this farm work now, but I do see evidence that it has been done because I see the products on the grocery shelves.

Fruits of Summer Labor

Summer is over and autumn is here. These past weeks I have enjoyed the fruits of the gardens of my nearby family and neighbors, as I have been the recipient of tomatoes, peppers, eggplant, zucchini, butternut squash and that wonderful tender lettuce which was perhaps a second planting.

I recall there was always a family garden when I was growing up. We had no rototillers or small garden plows and the garden patch was often prepared with a spade, hoe and rake. We siblings learned to drop two or three beans in a furrow, drop potato eyes in hills, and plant other small seeds as we did our part. The homegrown produce was always available in season and later on as home canned or stored food.

There was weeding and garden care to do, too. I remember that tomato vines had huge ugly green worms that ate the vines. Picking them off was a job we all tried to avoid. We also picked bugs off the potato plants, walking down the rows with a can of coal-oil in which to drop them. The thought of digging up under a potato plant and finding the light skinned vegetable was always amazing because we had nipped the potato bugs in their infancy.

We were obliged to do our stint at picking peas and beans. They had to be shelled and snapped. One of the favorite ways to prepare lettuce was to "wilt" it. Today it would be frowned on as it called for oil or bacon fat to make that tasty hot dressing. It really wilted the lettuce and with the addition of bits of bacon it was tasty.

It is hard to remember all the interests we had in our childhood that cost nothing. But there were many and we did find ways to pass the lazy summer days between school terms.

Nowadays if you are a child you must have a bed full of stuffed toys, board games, books, dolls, and neighborhood friends who come to play. Most kids have bicycles and roller blades or skate boards. But my siblings and I made our own entertainment.

Were those better days for us instead of what we see our children and grandchildren have today? I think so. We learned to be self-sufficient and were happy living without so many toys and/or the distraction of TV with its violence and horror series. It's back to the good old days for me.

Crocheted Hats as "Fancy" as it Gets

I never know what will turn out when I decide to nimble up my fingers with a crochet hook these days. As a youngster I had no domestic skills at all. The most "fancy work" as it was called then, that I did was to cross-stitch a little sample with turkey red thread from a small spool. As a matter of fact when I was a young woman it was customary to have a hope chest filled with linens and needs for a new home.

My dowry was two tea towels with a design (decal) that was ironed on and I did the cross stitching. Guess I didn't entertain much "hope." I thought I would be an LOPH (left on papa's hands) and didn't prepare for a marriage.

Back to the crocheting: A church circle I belonged to in another town was asked to use some yarn that had accumulated in the church storeroom and make granny squares to be sewn together for throws for nursing homes. I sat in on the instruction and went home with my quota of yarn. Sitting down one evening I began what I remembered of the instructions. No matter how I tried I never could make a square. My creations turned into round things that resembled little hats. So one evening as I was absent-mindedly crocheting and watching television I suddenly realized that I had fashioned a full blown hat. I never went back to granny squares again!

The next Christmas my little granddaughter was the recipient of 14 hats which had somehow started out as granny squares and ended up as headgear. On Christmas day we watched with humor as she modeled the hats. Later I learned that she liked one better than all the others and chose to wear it all winter long.

I am the kind of person who cannot sit and watch TV without doing something with my hands, and that is why I crochet. When my DAR chapter requested lap robes for the Veterans' Home here in Bennington I said I could do that and my project ended up with 77 multi-colored lap robes.

Usually I do marginal televiewing and sit and crochet. That is why I am turning out these strange and unusual hat creations. With tag ends of yarn in my basket I work them together in designs and odd shapes; no two are alike. I toss them in a bag and give them away. Maybe someone will see my hats on someone's head one of these cold days. It's possible that some store may market them, perhaps as a far-out item of apparel, or because they see something useful and unique in what I have put together with my crochet hook.

As a granny square maker, I'm a better hat maker!

Suddenly Swept Away

*A*s I looked at the havoc done by the flooding following Hurricane Floyd along the Atlantic coast I thought back to a period in the late 1940s when there was flooding in the Midwest where we lived. It was precipitated by heavy rains and with all the little streams feeding into the Big Muddy Missouri River, its overflow and flooding caused millions of dollars in damage. The little stream that ran through our town in Missouri went out of its banks, and people with rowboats went out to rescue people whose houses were on lower grounds. Our house sat on a hill and we watched the boat people oar down what was once a road to take the people to a shelter in the school.

When the waters receded we drove to areas where the damage was so extensive. The muck, mud, slime and stench after a flood is oppressive. We looked at the soilage and wondered if ever it could be cleaned up and places made habitable. Often those areas were just bulldozed and new houses and facilities sprang up in their place. New levees were built on the banks of the "Big Mo."

When you think of the treasures, furniture and appliances that are a total loss you shudder to think how you would feel if your possessions were suddenly swept away.

When I lived in Iowa as a child the little crick (that's what we called them in Iowa) would rise up almost to the bridge level; we thought that was a bad flood. Those swirling, eddying brown waters rushing under the bridge as we watched logs and all kinds of debris float by, were shocking. Little did I know that in later years I would witness several floods in places where I lived.

Someone asked me if I had ever been in a tornado. Not actually, but I do remember one night I spent with an uncle and aunt in the country in Cass County Iowa when we were awakened and urged to put on our sandals and go to the storm cellar. The wind was blowing very hard, the sky was aglow with rivers of lightning and it was a time of anxiety, and yes, excitement. We crowded into the storm cellar which was used to store canned vegetables and as a root cellar. There we huddled until my uncle called an all clear and we were able to return to our beds.

When I lived in Kansas I have seen funnel shaped clouds in the distance, but never actually experienced the havoc of these freaks of nature. I have viewed the damage they do on television and that is enough. And right here in North Bennington a few years ago, we had kind of a mini tornado that ripped through sections of our town.

The emotions of people who suffer these losses are varied. Some are very philosophical about it, others can't understand why it had to happen to them, and still others carry on so emotionally that you can almost feel their pain and loss.

Also weatherwise, I recall blizzards in the Midwest. One afternoon I stayed to clean the blackboard erasers by dusting them over a waste basket. That delayed my going home with my siblings. The snow began to come down very hard and before I could get to my home I was chilled to the bone, my overshoes were full of snow and I could hardly see in front of me. But I trudged on and finally stumbled almost frozen into the house.

There were no snowplows then, and roads were not opened except by what they called graders. Sidewalks were not shoveled as they are today. It didn't keep the schools closed as they were open the next day. Somehow the hardy Midwesterners knew how to cope with the elements and we trudged off to school with our long underwear and four buckled overshoes protecting us from what the weatherman gave to us.

Reflections on Our Veterans

Veterans Day has come and gone with local celebrations and national observances. At the local Veterans' Home and around the small towns of our area appropriate observations were held and participated in by veterans of the wars in which our young men — and women — fought.

When November 11, 1918 was first proclaimed Armistice Day because fighting had ceased in Europe, I was six years old. (I can hardly believe that 72 years have passed since that first Armistice Day was proclaimed.) But I do remember it as clearly as if it had happened yesterday. I didn't understand the meaning of it all, but I was swept along in the mass of school children who had been let out of the classrooms to go to the main street to move with the surging mass of people who were celebrating the cease fire.

In the little town in Iowa where I lived we had no paid fire department. We did have a municipal water works and what may have been then an up-to-date fire truck. There was no klaxon or warning signal that sounded when a fire was discovered, but in several places around town there were fire bells. They were usually placed atop a 20-foot high wooden structure with a huge bell with a rope pull. To signal a call to the volunteer fire fighters, someone would ring those bells.

Well, those few bells located around the neighborhoods rang out with loud clangs continually throughout November 11, 1918. Someone would take over when a volunteer's arm would tire. Always to signal a disaster, the bells this day were pealing a celebration. The surging masses of school children, townspeople, parents and country folks who came to town that day acclaimed the peace that had come; that terrible four-year war in Europe had ended.

More than a million American troops were in Europe in July 1918 and saw service before the war ceased on November 11. There was a total of 320,710 casualties according to the World Almanac.

One of the frightening and stark events of that day so long ago was the burning in effigy of the Kaiser. I did not know who the Kaiser was, as at six years of age I wasn't reading the newspaper; I was hardly beginning to read the Uncle Wiggly books. But the mob of people knew who the Kaiser was and the hooting and hollering and perhaps some inebriated performances were the order of the day.

Two of my uncles on my paternal side had served in that war. One came back from the trench war and was affected the rest of his life from the mustard gas effects. The soldiers of that war continued to wear their army issue clothing several months afterwards perhaps to show their patriotism. They looked strange in their olive drab gear with their wrapped puttees, but I think their pride that they had served their country made them want to wear their army clothes.

Armistice Day was officially changed to Veterans' Day in 1954 when it was designated to commemorate the end of hostilities in 1918 and 1945. Now it is a time we remember veterans of all wars in which our country has participated.

We were living on an Army Post at Fort Riley, Kansas when V-E Day was declared May 7, 1945 and also at the same place when V-J Day was announced August 14 the same year. It was not as rousing a celebration on the Post as was the 1918 observance in that little Iowa town.

Waiting to See What's Next

Eighty-eight years ago I first saw the light of day in a four-square house on the outskirts of a small Iowa town. I don't remember it of course, but my birth certificate indicates that it was a home confinement, the doctor's name was C.R. Jones and my mother was 34 years old. I was No. 5 in our large family of nine born in Iowa and Nebraska.

My name on the certificate was spelled with two "t"s but you note that I use the old English spelling of Harriette. There was never any legal changing of my name; I just added the extra "e" when I found that my maternal grandmother's name was spelled that way.

Over the past eight decades I had a jaunty, exciting and uncommonly interesting ride through life. I have lived through World Wars I and II, the Korean War, Vietnam and the Persian Gulf struggle. There have been two depressions: the stock market crash in the late 1920s and the sad, bad years of the '30s when hard times with dust storm on the Plains, unemployment, Conservation Corps, WPA projects and other happenings good and bad on the way up to the present good economy. Quite an historic panorama of events.

It has been my privilege to do a bit of national and foreign traveling. I have been blessed with two sons who are, incidentally, in the senior category. Truly for me now, these are the golden years.

I have seen the passing of five of my siblings, the oldest at age 96 last year. There are plans to get together with the four of us remaining siblings when we hold a reunion in Kansas in May. My oldest living sibling is 94, the next 90. I'm 88 and my brother is 81. And not an Alzheimer's victim in the bunch. We're looking forward to reminiscing about hard times, good times, old time customs and practices, heart-to-heart talks and perhaps we'll even indulge in some "true confessions."

This remarkable trip through these many decades have brought me blessing and distress. But isn't everybody's life made up of starts and stops, joys and sadnesses, exhilarations and down-times?

Now I'll just coast and see if there are more excitements, blessings and whatever, waiting in the wings.

May-Basket Memories

*M*ay is almost over but I want to recall May baskets of years ago. I noted in the *Bennington Banner* several letters to the editor mentioned surprise May baskets received and it reminded me of old time baskets my sisters and I used to make in this beautiful month of May.

We began making baskets two or three weeks ahead of the date. We used shoe boxes, oatmeal boxes and any kind of cardboard container that could be covered with crepe paper. The baskets were trimmed with various designs using braids, edging or different colored paper. They had a handle made out of construction paper as this was necessary for hanging them on door knobs.

Another kind of basket we made was an elongated cob-webby creation with tissue paper. It came in such delicate lovely colors; this is now used mostly for packing or wrapping gifts. We would fold the sheet diagonally and make alternating cuts leaving enough for a top gathering. When opened these were dripping pieces of art. When they were finished we would hang them on the lace curtains waiting for May Day.

The box baskets were always filled with spring flowers such as violets, lady slippers and dog-toothed violets which were gathered in the woods. The flowers were kept fresh in old Mason jars ready to be wrapped in cheesecloth to keep them fresh in the baskets.

When we began to make May baskets we were never allowed to use the good shears that our mother used for dressmaking (she made all our clothes). If we could not afford the library paste that came in a bottle with a screw top and a brush inserted in the top, we made our own paste with flour and water. It didn't stick as well but was effective.

The baskets were usually tagged for friends with our name on them. When the time came we carried our little arty things and placed them at the door or hung them on the knob of friends' houses. They were sort of a surprise token as I recall. Carrying the delicate, flimsy cob-webby ones was quite a feat if you had a number of friends. It was great fun and a springtime therapy to make these baskets, but more fun to come home and find we too had been remembered on May Day.

Another May event was winding the Maypole. This was usually done at the end of the school year which always ended in May. Crepe paper streamers were attached to a tall pole, and each child held the streamer and was instructed to wend their way around so that when the children came together close to the pole, they had made a lovely braided, colorful effect.

O lovely May! It stirred long ago memories.

Putting the "Express" in Express Mail

$\mathcal{B}$ack in the days when we used to write letters we would write our return address in the upper left hand corner of the envelope. Sometimes it was fashionable to write it on the back of the envelope flap and not clutter up the address side. Printed labels were not heard of then, and only firms had envelopes with printed return addresses.

When I think about letters, packages, and return addresses I remember the little post office in the small Nebraska town where I lived. We had a postmistress and two rural mail carriers. Sometimes she would let my sister and me go behind all those combination lock mailboxes and "distribute" the mail. What grown-up fun! At the close of the business day the postmistress — her name was Inez — would put the outgoing mail in a pouch, take it to the railroad depot and hang it on a pole. It was always done just before the flyer from Omaha came through around four o'clock. As the train sped — at a little slower speed — an arm would shoot out from the mail car and snatch that mail pouch. And the local mail was on its way.

I visited the railroad museum in Sacramento a few years ago and one of the exhibits was the mail car. Railroad workers rode the train and sorted the mail that was picked up from those arms or off the loading station platforms. In this old time railroad exhibit I saw how mail was sorted while the train was speeding down the track. Two dozen or so mail bags were lined up with signs designating areas of the country or large cities. Four or five dispatchers would work on each mail car. I saw the apparatus, or arm, that shot out from the mailcar to grab those mail pouches that little towns used to send mail on its way.

Nowadays mail is transported in trucks locally or regionally but airplanes carry the cross country postals. I'm a steady user of the U.S. mail and their Priority Mail is an excellent service. I'm amazed to find that it costs only a few cents more to send Priority Mail instead of Parcel Post. There is such a service as Overnight Priority Mail. My son in California mailed me a package airmail express recently, and it was delivered to my door just 24 hours later.

Heavens! What changes we have had over the years. There are not a lot of letter writers such as we had 75 years ago. But junk mail and commercial advertisers keep postal employees busy these days. I rather like to think of the simple, unhurried days when that little post office pouched the mail for pick up by the fast flyer out of Omaha.

Old-fashioned Treats

Looking at a Vermont Country Store catalog made me think about penny candy. Most cities and large towns many years ago had a Five and Dime store. In the little Iowa town where I was a youngster there was a "Fair" store. It had all kinds of retail items, but in the front of the store was the penny candy counter. My girl chum always seemed to have a few pennies or a nickel tucked away in a dress pocket and we made a daily stop at the front counter on the way home from school.

I remember the Necco wafers which came in a tube-like wrap with all colors of round flat pieces. They could be easily parceled out one at a time and had various flavors. Jawbreakers always fascinated me; as you licked off one layer there was another beneath it of a different color. Those things were hard and you couldn't share one after you put it in your mouth, but one often took it out to see what color had come up. It could actually break your jaw if you tried to bite through it!

How about those old-fashioned chocolate creams which were cone shaped! The chocolate covering concealed maple, lemon, orange, vanilla and strawberry flavors, and you could get several of them for a nickel.

And yes, those Nonpareils. The story about this candy treat is that when Etienne Guittard went to San Francisco in the mid 1800s he couldn't make it in the gold fields, but made his fortune by the chocolate candy route. His concoction was a one inch flat drop of chocolate covered with white pellets of sugar — or sprinkles as we know them today.

And do you remember Sen Sen that was put under the tongue? It was a little candy bit that had a strong licorice flavor which people used as breath fresheners. I loathed the smell of it, but it was the thing way, way back when. Best beaux often showed up with a Sen Sen breath!

I remember those long licorice sticks which were twisted in about a 15-inch length. Today they come in various lengths. The Fair store also had those miniature glass cars and trains with little sugar pellets in them. They lasted a long time, one at a time.

Jordan almonds were a particular favorite of mine, but they weren't really in the penny candy class. They are a hard sugar coated piece concealing a whole almond; you sucked on the coating until you got down to the almond to enjoy the best part of this sweetmeat.

The Vermont Country Store catalog mentioned other candies such as peppermint patties, Goo Goos (with peanut butter), Valomilks that were poured into milk chocolate cups, chocolate butter almond toffee, and the original salt water taffy.

Salt water taffy happened this way according to the ad in the Country Store catalog: In Atlantic City in 1885 Fralingers Candy Store introduced the original salt water taffy. Fralinger's goodie was soft enough so it didn't pull on your teeth and was chewy enough so the full flavor lingered. I don't know if Fralingers is still in business but most any shore boardwalk sells salt water taffy today.

That Vermont Country Store can bring back all those old time candy treats as they stock them, if you oldsters get a hunger for them.

Welcome Home, and Back Again

I have just returned from the Midwest where I attended a family reunion. Only four of us siblings are left but we gathered with sons, nieces, nephews and grands at the home of a niece in Fairview, Kansas and looked back 70 plus years.

The family included my 94-year-old sister from Nebraska who carried a cane which she used as an attention-getter as well as her support. She was dressed up in a well-tailored suit, costume jewelry, rouge and lipstick. Oh yes, she had a hearing aid which she kept adjusting to catch all that was being said. My next sister from Colorado who is 90 was there with sons from Colorado and British Columbia; she managed to amaze us all as she is almost blind. I was next in line and then my 80-year-old brother was there from Illinois.

We drove to the little Kansas and Nebraska towns where we grew up. What a shock! The little berg in Nebraska was almost obliterated and the Kansas road sign counted a population of 252. A passerby was engaged in conversation to learn if anyone was still around who would remember our family. There was nary a glimmer of recollection. After all, 77 years would wipe out three generations and we should not have been disappointed. Perhaps we should have gone to the cemetery to check on former neighbors!

The son of my older brother who died at age 30 was there and I tried to see some resemblance to this sibling who died so young; there was none.

The school house in two of the little towns had been torn down and the church where I was married was torn down. Store fronts were boarded up; the main drags looked like a toothless old woman where fire had wiped out structures or they had been razed. What seemed to us as large houses when we were young appeared squat, square and miniature now. The house we lived in had been torn down and the big drainage ditch in front was filled in and grassed over. The big house across the street with the beautiful lawn which Vince Arnold mowed when the dew was still on the grass, was the site of a double garage. We noted a lot of trailer homes.

When it came time to say goodbye we siblings knew this might be the last time we would see each other. Even though we obviously have good genes as our 94, 90, 88 and 80 years of age attest, we felt that we would "never pass this way again."

The midwestern landscape was so foreign to me after living in Vermont. You could see for miles and miles and acres and acres of terraced farm land was planted with corn, soybeans and grains. Big old two story with attic farm houses have been replaced with low ranches. An outstanding feature was the big metal storage bins, sometimes as many as four of five on a farm. Shelled grain is stored and each has a moisture control which is automatic to keep the grain dry and marketable.

The creeks and rivers were very dry and even the Missouri which we crossed four times en route to Kansas from Illinois, had many sand bars. One river, the Wabash which is the dividing line between Indiana and Illinois seemed to be running full. We crossed by car the Cannonball Bridge near Vincennes where the old railroad train, the Wabash Cannonball used to cross the river.

Going back to the midwest was a trip down memory lane, but it doesn't compare to the welcome sight of Vermont's Green Mountains.

Wherever You Go,
It's Still Home Cooking

*I*t's a meat-and-potatoes-and-gravy world out there and you often get caught in it when you choose to eat out. Such was — and is — my experience not just in this area, but I encountered it recently in the Midwest. Joining siblings and other relatives in reunion we wanted to eat our meals together and sought places where our big crowd could be accommodated.

One of these places was the Cozy Cafe in a little town in Kansas. It was a small operation, but I do believe all the old folks eat their meals there at noon. We arrive around 11:30 and the place began to fill up.

The tables were covered with vinyl or simple paper place mats. The menu was written on a board high above the counter in two places. That meant that the menu was changed every day. No printed menus covered with food particles and greasy fingerprints — just specials of the day and no fast food!

Our raucous, happy bunch settled at tables that had been squeezed together to accommodate us. A senior waitress came with her plain little note pad to take our orders. We had several choices but each one included king-sized midwestern helpings of potatoes and gravy. The sectional plates were filled to overflowing with the other choices.

With 11 of us we thought we would surely confuse the waitress. She returned rather quickly with our meals, each one set precisely at the right place. They served a little dish of fruited jello first. This didn't come in a can! The meat entree tasted homemade but the peas, corn, beans and applesauce may have come from a can. The carrots were fresh cooked and there was no green salad.

The menu board showed four special desserts, one of them being fresh strawberry pie. Obviously this was a favorite because by the time we got around to ordering dessert the waitress had reached up and erased that item. We had to settle for another homemade pie.

We could see the cook who was dishing up the food at the pass-through window. She appeared to be a senior too but was not rattled, nor overwhelmed by the deluge of orders coming in. She did have a rather large ladling spoon though, as our plates attested.

By noon I think all the senior citizens were clamoring for a place in the little restaurant. It might have seated 60 patrons in booths, tables and counter space. It was probably a "mom and pop" enterprise or two older gals running a successful eatery. But only at lunchtime.

Naturally our group was having a good time and we were a bit hilarious about some jokes and remembrances. One booth patron came over to our table and asked where we were from. "Why, we're from all over," said our spokesman. And the retired farmer (obviously) said, "I didn't think you were from around here."

And so it was. Meat, potatoes, gravy, fresh cooked veggies and homemade pies. Not great diet stuff but tasty and hearty. Guess things haven't changed all that much since I left the Midwest over 50 years ago.

How the Paper Gets to Us

*I*n a recent issue of the *Bennington Banner* they printed a display ad to tell the "remarkable story" of how their paper got into your hands. It stated that the "paper is put to bed, machines start to roll, presses print 55,000 newspapers at a speed of 25 miles an hour; newspapers are loaded into 15 vehicles with excellent shock absorbers traveling a half million miles a year; drivers take the papers to more than 100 stores and 70 vending machines, and 40 carriers deliver 10,000 papers to 1,000 doorsteps and front porches."

The paper has also printed stories about their carriers and I too applaud them. My carrier tosses it on my deck so that I can reach out and get it with one grasp.

That's particularly helpful in the winter when the snow blankets my driveway and makes the footing unsure, because my newspaper box is a hundred feet away from my house.

That's a neat story but I think back to the time when my husband and I were publishing four little weekly papers in the Midwest. Putting the paper to bed was a laborious task as we struggled with outdated linotypes and presses. All the news gathering, printing, bookkeeping and other tasks were done by us and a printer's devil. The old printing press we used was called a Chicago Stop Press. As it rolled the paper over the forms of type a fly wheel on the back caught the paper and flung it down with a sharp thud and stopped! Yes, it actually stopped and we wondered if it would continue its cycle. I guess that is why it is called a Chicago Stop Press! However, it did begin to come to life and went through the cycle as before. No 55,000 revolutions back in those days!

But that old press was not with us long. It gave up the ghost before we did and a second hand Chandler and Price was acquired and we went on with printing our little weekly efforts.

I'm trying to remember how many subscribers we had and I believe it would number around 300 to 500 for each paper. We loaded the bundles in our arms and carried them to the post office a block away.

Those for the other three towns were driven in our old 1935 Chevy to the nearby post offices. We traveled perhaps about 65 miles in our circuit, sometimes late at night as that is when we completed our editions.

We had no vending machines, or carriers. In little towns the local post office was our distributor along with the rural free delivery route carriers.

Our little country weeklies were eagerly awaited by our subscribers. I believe the price of a subscription was $1.50 a year.

Sometimes we would offer a special rate around the holidays of $1 per year. Can you imagine: 52 issues for $1? Well, that's what it was. And when I think of the sweat and struggle and the fury we leveled at our antiquated equipment I can hardly believe we endured the game.

The *Banner* ad made it all sound simple and easy. I hope that when you read your paper every day you appreciate having a local "rag." Technology has made publishing easier, but not necessarily less laborious. The strenuous obstacles we faced more than a half century ago to get the news to our readers were a real challenge. I hope you appreciate your local news source.

Back to School

I had more than a bird's eye view a few days ago when I went with my daughter-in-law to carry the gear my granddaughter needs for her college dorm room. It was a hands-on operation and I was permitted to carry one bag up to the third floor single room.

My, my, my! I didn't realize what it takes to go to college these days. This is my granddaughter's second year at St. Lawrence University in Canton, N.Y. and we made the trip on a bright, warm August day. The family van was loaded with such items as a microwave, toaster oven, small refrigerator, book cases, a collapsible futon with pad; plastic crates for shelving; a 6 x 9 rug, electric fan, suitcases of clothes; packages of tea, cocoa, snackies, laundry detergent, first aid items, and clothes on hangers. My granddaughter went up the day before with a computer and the necessities for the first overnight, and her stereo.

Every student room I passed had a computer on the desk — which are designed for such equipment. Actually the only furniture in the room when my granddaughter arrived was a bureau with deep drawers, a single bed and the computer desk and a chair. When we left after carrying all the gear up three flights the room looked like a small efficiency apartment.

The beautiful part is that my granddaughter looked forward eagerly to her second year in college and was happy to pack up and get back to the books. She has made us proud by making the dean's list her first year thus qualifying for a single room. We expect her to achieve and graduate with honors.

A half century or more ago when one went off to college they could probably carry all their clothes in a hard-backed suitcase. There would be no eating in the dorms like today except a candy bar or a Care package from home. Potato chips were a possibility then, too.

Linens were provided by the colleges and each room may have had two or three occupants. Maybe one of them would have had to sleep in a bunk bed. Each student had a desk and a set of drawers and hanging space on the wall. The floors were likely inlaid linoleum or plain wooden floors.

Students in those days carried their books in their arms. No bookbags or backpacks like today. I don't believe as many books were required as the library was the resource center. Today, the computer can supply so much. Also I spoke to a second year student who was "sweating" about the cost of his first semester books — $325. Wow! A half century ago that would have been enough to buy books through a whole college undergraduate level.

It was very evident as I looked around the campus that the usual mode of wear was cut off jeans, sweat shirts, baggy pants and sandals. Actually I saw some barefooted students because it was a warm day. But whatever the wear, they all looked intent — to get an education. The first two days were for setting up their rooms. I'm hoping that all that gear that is provided for the students will result in making it easy for them to feel comfortable and want to study and achieve the goal they have set out to achieve.

Rah! Rah! Rah!

A Rite of Passage

Tomorrow is the day all Americans should get out and vote. I have been voting a long time and would never forfeit my right of franchise, particularly in the presidential election. I cast my first such vote in Kansas in the deepest Depression years and voted for Herbert Hoover and Charles Curtis.

You had to be 21 before you could vote 68 years ago! I turned 21 in April and was qualified to vote in the November election. It was a proud moment when I asked for my ballot. I have never missed voting in a presidential election in all these years. One year I was traveling Down Under but cast my absentee vote before I departed the country.

These days citizens can vote at age 18. The 26th Amendment passed in 1971 granted the right of franchise to all 18-year-olds. If they were old enough to fight for their country they were old enough to vote. Young voters can have an important impact on the election outcome. There are so many sources of information and they should know what is going on in the world today. Or do they pay attention? I read about a poll where some young people didn't even know who was running for president.

When I voted the first time in that little Kansas town, the polling place was in a section of a business office. Two little curtained cubicles were set up so that a secret ballot could be cast. When the polls closed a staid group of citizens closeted themselves and counted the ballots by hand tally. I remember one time I had the privilege of helping count ballots in Massachusetts. It was a laborious task in the 1960s as each vote was tallied on a big sheet and then counted. The winners were not divulged until 2 or 3 a.m. the next day. It was a learning experience for me. Since then, machines have taken over the counting.

I first voted by machine in Delaware and pulled a lever to indicate my preference. I was quite flummoxed by the mechanics of it and had to ask for help. I eventually made my choice in the secret booth.

One presidential election that left an impact on me was in 1936. We lived near the home of the Republican nominee, Alfred G. Landon. My husband and I were among the many who milled around the governor's mansion in Topeka the night of the election. We were waiting for Gov. Landon and his wife Theo to come out on the front veranda and hear his acceptance speech and become the next president-elect of the United States. Of course he did not win, losing to Franklin D. Roosevelt who went on to be elected president four times.

Other voting experiences flit back into my memory. I have lived and voted in several different states in my long life. Wherever we resided I exercised my right to vote for elected officials or proposals. I urge all citizens to line up, take their ballot and vote in secret for your favorite candidates. It is our inalienable right and we should not forfeit the opportunity to exercise it.

When Flu Was a Terror

The *Wellness Connection* is a communication that comes out monthly from Southwestern Vermont Health Care. The November issue has just reached me and its lead article is about colds, pneumonia and flu. That set me to thinking what I remembered about that Spanish flu epidemic that hit our country back in 1918. It infected about half the world's population claiming 20 million lives which was more casualties than all of World War I.

We were living in Iowa when that scourge hit and I was six years old. The war was ending but the flu epidemic held terror for the population. That was in the days when a family would be quarantined if there was measles, smallpox, scarlet fever or other communicable diseases. Not so the flu, as I remember. In our home there were several family members who were ill with the flu and the living room became like a ward in a hospital. Several beds were moved into that sizable room. My mother who was a strong woman was the "nurse" to the sick patients. We children were not allowed into that room, and fortunately none of us contracted the disease.

Our play activities had to be in other parts of the house. A very poignant reminder of those activities was something that happened to me. We had rigged up some chairs with table boards which we were using for bridges or hurdles to jump over. When my turn came to jump one of the boards slipped off the rung and I landed on the corner of a chair.

The result was a gash between my eyes. Blood started streaming down my face and I ran screaming, thinking I was going to die. Death from the flu was a constant but I thought I would die from all that blood that was running down my face. I thought I was mortally wounded.

My mother left the care of the flu patients and called my father who came home to look after me. He bundled me up and carried me to the doctor's office. It was determined that I would need to be "stitched up." While that was going on I was yelling my 6-year-old head off.

Actually it didn't hurt that much to have the stitches put in, and the procedure was over in a short while.

Of course I healed and also survived a flu attack along with my other siblings. It wasn't deliberate to add my little accident to the deep concern of the sick flu patients in our home, but it happened. I still carry that scar to this day. That's what I remember of the 1918 flu epidemic.

An admonition: flu is a serious concern every year and if you haven't had your shot, you'd better check the agencies where you can be vaccinated. Flu can be prevented with the annual vaccination. It's just not for the elderly, but for health care workers and every one. Better get your flu shot.

Remembering Mother

I was touched by what *Bennington Banner* Publisher Joe Karius wrote about his mother at her death recently. She was just a year older than I am when she passed away. I applaud Joe for extolling his mother's virtues. She lived during the Depression years and Joe told that story as it pertained to her. The praise of his mother's fine hand in his upbringing was very moving.

It reminded me of my mother's caring ways. With a large family, how she managed to look after all of us amazes me as I reflect on her life. She didn't live to be as old as Joe's mother, passing away at age 69.

We oldsters remember our mothers as caregivers. They did not have time to work outside the home. It was a full time job to attend to the needs and wants of a family. I can still feel the soothing comfort of a warm soft cloth sponging away the fever in my body. And the spooning of warm soup into my mouth when I was sick. I look backward at some of the home remedies my mother used. Some were unpleasant to us. One was the custom of wearing a little bag of asafetida around our necks. It was a gum resin of oriental plants which was a folk remedy against disease. We children were always a little embarrassed by the string around our necks and the offensive smell. Another old time practice was drinking sassafras tea that was deemed important usually in the spring time.

There were many commonplace ministrations done by my mother which linger in my mind. Seeing that we had clean clothes, what were then considered nutritious meals, household chores and certain restrictions on things we shouldn't do. My mother's method of punishment with a little whip around the legs stung just enough to remind us that we should not overstep that line again. The switch or twig was an old-fashioned way of discipline then.

My mother was always helpful to neighbors in home confinements. It is what is known now as midwifery. She was called out at all hours and would dutifully go to lend her help. She also nursed our skinned knees, took splinters out of hands, wrapped cloth bandages on cuts, and was our consoler when we had aches and pains. I remember her admonition as she referred to "growing pains."

My mother made all our clothes on a treadle Home rotary sewing machine. They were often handed down from child to child, sometimes needing a "letting out" or "hemming up" to make them fit. We learned to iron, did our part in the family washing which took place every Monday morning rain or shine; learned to sweep floors, dust, clean cupboards, mend, make beds, and do menial household chores. My sisters learned to cook but I was spared this chore because I had no aptitude for it; I always managed to find something else to do away from the cook stove.

Mothers today don't have that kind of time to spend with their children. Our mothers did most of the "upbringing," and the many lessons I learned at "my mother's knee" drift back as I reflect on her life.

So as Joe Karius eulogized and blessed his 89-year-old mother a few weeks ago, I pay tribute to my mother who also possessed those redeeming maternal tendernesses and attributes.

Fruits of the Past

I was peeling apples for a dessert one day last week and when I saw the pile of parings left in the sink I thought about what my grandmother would have done with them instead of putting them in the disposal. Back in those days on the farm nothing was ever thrown away. There was no garbage to compost. The apple peelings would have been boiled to get the pectin and color from the skins and then processed into jelly. Jellies you buy today never taste like those my grandmother — or all farm women — made from what we toss away today.

I recall that my grandparents who lived on an Iowa farm had several apple trees from which they gathered their drop. They had an apple peeler which was hooked onto the kitchen table and after sticking the apple on the pronged fork you turned a handle and it peeled the apple perfectly. They also had a cherry pitter which I thought was a neat gadget.

In the midwest there were a lot of "sour" cherry trees and I picked many a bucket of them as we climbed the low trees to get at them. They had a cherry pitter into which you dropped handfuls of washed fruit. It was necessary to have a pan to catch the juice as the fruit was pitted.

My grandmother was a stern Quaker woman who presided over these food processings. When she canned cherries she always threw a pit or two in each jar. There was a reason but I don't recall what it was unless it was to remind one that they were real fruit and a cherry pie that didn't yield a pit was unusual. Not too good on the teeth, but somehow there was always that one pit in her pies.

When we children visited our grandparents on the farm we would sit down at a table covered with a linen cloth and be served our meals.

There were those chunks of homemade butter slathered on baked potatoes. Sometimes potatoes were served with the jackets on. Who says those folks didn't know about healthy eating! If there were strawberries they were served with thick heavy cream which was brought up from the shed built over a spring where foods could be kept cool.

There was a machine that was used to separate the milk from the cream. It was an appliance that had a lot of movable parts with a huge tublike container into which the milk was poured as it was brought from the barn after milking. A crank turned the machinery and somehow going through all those parts the cream was separated from the milk. The cream (and milk) were sold to creameries.

The chore of washing those separator parts was laborious; each had to be dried thoroughly before assembling for the next operation. Night and morning this separator was used to process the milk.

I started out with apples and ended up with milk. That was the way it was back on the farms long ago. Farm life today is a far cry from those days. I'm sure my grandparents were happy and industrious as they went about their daily tasks.

The Man Who Came with Chocolates

When I went to see "The Man Who Came to Dinner" at Old-castle Theatre recently, I remembered that I saw that production on stage in Topeka, Kansas in 1939. The Topeka Women's Club sponsored a matinee performance and I was privileged to attend.

In telling Daryl Kenny (one of the Oldcastle cast) that I had seen the play over 60 years ago, she gasped and said that I must have seen Alexander Woollcott who did the original role in this classic Moss Hart and George S. Kaufman play. I did! Woollcott was known in literary circles as a conversationalist and raconteur of great charm and he played "the man" superbly. Incidentally Willy Jones did a fine acting job of "the man" at Oldcastle.

I was a green country girl and this was perhaps the first theatrical performance I had seen. In one scene "the man" was offered a chocolate from a Whitman's Sampler. That reminded me of how my older sisters used to get boxes of bon bons from their beaux. They often came courting with candy, not necessarily Whitman's. All chocolates have that same delicious aroma when you open a box. If my sisters offered me a piece it was hard to make up my mind about whether to choose a nutty goody, a caramel, a cherry covered with chocolate or a nougat piece.

Russell Stover was another popular brand long ago. The factory was in Kansas City and it was often the choice of the beaux. Recently I read that Stover and Whitman's joined their companies but still carry their individual name on their products.

It is at this time of year that friends of mine who live in Hamburg, Germany send me a package filled with European chocolate dainties. Along with the candy comes some delicate handmade Christmas ornament. This friendly association began a number of years ago when the husband was a post-doctoral intern at DuPont in Wilmington, Delaware. We met through a church affiliation and shared many happy times together despite the difference in our ages. They visited us later in the states but returned to Germany to make their permanent home and raise their two sons.

But back to the chocolates and my sisters' beaux. One could always tell if the romance was ripening according to the size of the box of candy. The number of layers in the box determined the ardor.

It's still a nice treat to receive my gift from Europe. My beaux during the depression didn't bring candy. Seeing that box of Whitman's Sampler at Oldcastle brought on all these memories. I'll have to take my treats in these golden years from dear young friends who were like family. I can't wait for this year's offering!

Trying Something Special

You're never too old to have one last fling at something special. That something for me came December 14, 2000 when I was privileged to offer my first effort in publishing a book. It took place at the local bookstore where they displayed copies and invited the public to purchase a book and have it signed by me.

A "book signing" was a new thing for me, but then there are many things I haven't experienced in this lifetime. One of my friends said she had never been to a book signing and thought it was a good time to attend mine. Actually a "signing" isn't any more than just that. I sat at a little table and signed my name on the header page. If it was someone "special" I wrote a little blurb with my signature.

When I read that First Lady Hillary Clinton had received an $8 million advance on a book, I realized how insignificant my little 88-page offering is. She is writing for a big publisher like Simon & Schuster. She will receive that $8 million before the book is ever written. With her backlog of experiences, recollections and happenings in the White House, and the high technology in computers and publishers, she will turn out a best seller.

I didn't aspire to best seller category. I just wanted to record some humorous — and some serious — happenings in my long life. I hope they wear well with the older generation in Vermont and surrounding areas. I didn't have to think about avoiding details that Hillary will likely have to contend with.

Writing is a pastime for me and fills my hours. It keeps my fingers nimble (at my trusty typewriter). I delve into my brain cells and pull out little nuggets of events and happenings in my long life. It does, however, rob me of hours of sleep at night as I mull over what I would like to write. If I don't set them down on paper when they surface they have flown right out of my head by daylight.

As I travel through these later years, a little nudge reminds me of something that took place years ago. Even though I have kept a journal for several decades (say like five) I don't refer to them all that much. Events and ideas have a way of trickling into my consciousness and I have to record them.

This winter will be a busy time for me as I sit at my window, glance at the snowy landscape, see the tracks in my driveway the *Banner* carrier makes when he leaves my paper on the deck, watch the birds seeking a seed or two to fuel their little feathered bodies, and do my thing at writing little essays.

Operator, Give Me Long Distance

When I talked to my California son the other day he asked me why I had not written about old-time telephones. I have given that some thought and now I'm ready to say something about this wonderful communication invention. My son informed me that he even remembered the number of the newspaper where I worked when we lived in Missouri. He recited it and said it was like knowing your name when you got lost. If he returned home from school before I arrived home he was to call *The Daily Standard*.

Thomas Alva Edison invented the first telephone in 1876. Since he was born in 1847, he was only 29 when this invention came about. The first telephone exchange was opened in New Haven, Connecticut in 1878 and Edison founded The Edison Electric Light Co. in October of that year.

On one of our travels through the Midwest we saw a sign pointing to the birthplace of Edison in Milan, Ohio. We made a detour to see this modest brick dwelling and entered the room where he was born. Milan was noted for the big homes that shipping magnates built; they were mansions compared to the house where Edison was born.

My first recollection of the telephone was an elongated box that hung on the wall. A speaking cone stuck out from the upper part and on one side there was a little handle that you cranked to call "Central." A little shelf jutted out from the long box where a note pad could be placed. You gave Central your number after you had picked up the receiver on the other side of the box. It was hung on a hook and looked like a hard rubber upside-down tumbler with a cord of about two feet.

There weren't many telephone owners back in the 1920s that I recall. The numbers were small and our house number was 2-4-8. No area codes, no long numbers, just crank to call "Central." She sat at a switchboard and when your call came in she made a connection to your party by pulling a plug from the depths of the switchboard and placing it in a particular hole. Then some little levers were pressed to activate your call. I always felt that Central had a very important job as throughout those early years they performed a necessary part of our communication field.

Old-fashioned phones hung on the wall. Since the receiver cord was not very long you could not sit down and carry on a conversation. Phones were used mostly for emergencies and to remind someone to bring something from the store on the way home from work. I was told that farm women would pick up the receiver and listen on the line, as there was no privacy in the early days.

From the old wall type phone they branched out to a stand-up unit with the receiver and speaking cone all in one piece. Later the squat style with the round dial on front came into use. Now we have that ubiquitous cell phone which you see glued to the ears of people on the street, in their cars, on planes and oh just everywhere.

We thank you Thomas Alva Edison for making all this possible with your simple little invention way back in 1878.

A Handkerchief Full of Memories

The other day while chatting with a friend I saw her take a hankie out of her sleeve and tend to her nose. I immediately was reminded of my fourth-grade teacher back in Iowa; she always carried a hankie tucked in her sleeve. Nowadays you hardly ever see anyone use a handkerchief; if they they have a cold they carry around a box of Kleenex.

My fourth-grade teacher's name was Etta Scharf. She was a rather buxom maiden lady who lived with a maiden sister and two brothers in a house near the school. One of the brothers, Otto, worked in the butcher shop. He was a hefty fellow and could easily lift a side of beef out of the cooler and cut off whatever you wanted. Sawdust covered the work area behind the display case of meat. I can see him swinging a long butcher knife against a whetstone sharpening it to easily cut the meat. His long white apron was stained with blood.

My teacher, Etta, wore her hair parted in the middle in a kind of twisted or braided style; perhaps she even wore "rats" to give it a pouf. Her apparel was a long black skirt and white blouse with a high neck. There was a little watch pinned on her ample chest which she looked at throughout the day. Her sturdy black oxfords had rubber heels so we never knew when she was walking around checking our study habits.

When we came into our classroom we were asked to sit quietly at our desk with folded hands until school "took up." We began the day with the Pledge of Allegiance. The pledge that we recited then was written especially for children in the summer of 1892 to commemorate that year's celebration of Columbus Day in public schools throughout the nation.

It first appeared in print September 8, 1892, the author being Francis Bellamy, editor of *The Youth's Companion*. Its popularity among the nation's school children and teachers made it into an annual Columbus Day tradition, then into a daily classroom ritual.

Two alterations have been made in the one I learned. In 1923 the somewhat ambiguously personal "my flag" was changed to "the flag of the United States of America." And in 1954 President Eisenhower signed a bill that introduced a religious note with the addition of the words "under God." I always have to stop and think where to insert that phrase because years ago I learned it otherwise.

After reciting the Pledge of Allegiance we all stood beside our desks and did a little calisthenics routine. Our curriculum included Readin', Ritin' and 'Rithmetic (now math), geography, history, art and music. We had recesses morning and afternoon. The sandy playground had sparse apparatuses and I can remember only the swings and teeter totters. The first kids out got them while the others had supervised playground activities. It was a full day from 8 in the morning until 4 in the afternoon.

Funny, what memories a single mannerism such as using a hankie can call to mind. I still keep hankies to be used at weddings and funerals.

The Treasurer and Me

When I read the story in the *Bennington Banner* the other day about the counterfeit $20 bills that were circulating our area I decided to take a closer look. The one in my billfold had a red mark on the left side and a number written in pencil on the right side. I have no idea what those markings meant but I'm sure there was some reason for such designation.

I also looked at the signature of the Treasurer of the United States which is on every piece of currency issued by our government. It was Mary Ellen Withrow's. Her name appears on one side of all bills and Robert Rubin, Secretary of the Treasury, on the opposite side. No doubt they will be replaced by someone in the new administration and in due time we will see different signatures on both sides of our bills.

A long time ago the name that appeared on all United States currency was that of Georgia Neese Clark. She was appointed as treasurer by President Roosevelt as she was a staunch follower of that party. You wonder why I brought this up. Here's my story:

When my first husband and I were struggling to establish a little chain of weekly papers in Kansas, one of those papers came about through the urging of Georgia Neese Clark. She was the banker in a little town south of us and thought they could support a little weekly. Since she was a source of inspiration to those 200 souls in that little berg, we began publishing the *Richland News*.

When we sold our newspapers after five years we moved to Topeka, then into army life and back to Topeka for a few years. We learned that Georgia Neese Clark was living in Topeka so we got together for a visit. We reviewed our struggle to supply her little town with a paper, and also caught up on other activities.

Georgia Neese Clark was a strikingly beautiful woman. She was a bit above the normal height for women and had an impressive personality. (Her mother, incidentally, was a relative of the woman who wrote little items for our paper in our main plant. I guess that had something to do with how we came to know her.) Georgia was our benefactor — not in a financial way — but in terms of urging us to expand our little publishing enterprise.

I recall that every Friday morning we drove the little bundle of papers 12 miles to Richland. The little post office in a general store disbursed the copies (four tabloid pages) to the one rural route carrier and the few boxholders. In the wintertime as we drove our delivery we noted the smoke curling from the chimneys where early morning fires were warming the homes. It was a simple, serene vista and it sort of warmed our hearts to know that our little publication would be read in those homes.

Strange, what memories are stirred by reading about a counterfeit $20 bill. But there they are and that's my story for today.

Seeing Red Over Green Ketchup

A day or so ago I read that Heinz company is introducing the unthinkable — green ketchup. Can you believe that? The 131-year-old food manufacturer had to do something to counteract their dropping to about 43 percent of the U.S. ketchup market in the late 1990s and have resorted to green ketchup.

The article states that the new green product tastes just like the old red stuff even though it is the color of spinach. Their new product squirts a stream so kids can dribble it over their burgers and fries in an artistic way.

It states that you could count on the sky being blue, grass growing green and ketchup pouring out red. But GREEN. I think I'll have a little trouble with that icky color.

I recall seeing how ketchup was made back in the old days. I saw how that spicy condiment was cooked and preserved for winter use. There was a big caldron set on a tripod over a wooden fire out in the open. The bountiful harvest of garden tomatoes were peeled by scalding off the skins and then plopped into a big iron kettle over the flames. Spices were added and the long simmering process to cook out the juices began.

Of course it was necessary to stir and stir the liquid as it plop-plopped and bubbled to the right consistency. A long handled spoon or homemade gadget was used because one had to stand back from the fire.

It was a day-long job to make that huge batch of red stuff. French fries were never heard of then, so the smooth-textured homemade condiment was used in meat loaves and casseroles and baked beans.

Ketchup was also called catsup then, and the making usually took place in late July or August when tomatoes were picked by the bushels. I helped slip the skins off the scalded tomatoes when I visited the farm and it was a hot job. Standing over that boiling, simmering huge iron kettle outside and stirring was also a hot job.

Nowadays ketchup is always on the table when you dine out, or for cookouts. You can have all the green ketchup they can manufacture but for me, I'll take the good old kind that comes out of the bottle red. I remember an old time verse when ketchup was so thick it would not flow out of the bottle: "Shake, shake, shake the bottle, none will come and then a lot'll." I suppose the green stuff will have a different consistency since it flows, but I'll think twice before I buy a bottle of it.

Greatest Accomplishments

I always read obituaries in the newspaper. One never knows when you will find that an illustrious person has passed away. There are lots of distinguished people who come to this area to retire and I find it interesting to read about their accomplishments.

There are those who leave their mark on the minds of people for simple little acts. One was Ada Horton who died at age 98. She was remembered for the fine dinner rolls she made for food sales.

That is a rare accomplishment and I picture the fine featherlight rolls that must have come from her kitchen. It reminded me of a favorite Aunt Kitty whose claim to fame was her light dinner rolls. Whenever the family had a get together we always counted on Aunt Kitty bringing her dinner rolls. I tried to make them from her recipe but they didn't turn out like hers. It was a gift and I'm sure that Ada Horton had that way with yeast, flour and shortening.

Aunt Kitty also made delicious chocolate cake. I can see her sitting at the family table with her little pince-nez glasses, beaming at her offering to the meal. When her husband died she broke up her home and I was the recipient of many of her treasured articles. Chief among them was her collection of dainty china tea cups, which started me on a collection spree. She also gave me her fine crystal goblets which were so fragile I almost hated to use them.

Please don't think I'm peculiar because I read obituaries. It's just that as older people — and sometimes young ones — pass away we learn of their contribution to the lives of those around them.

You never know about them until you read their obituary.

I hope that families will continue to remember the particular activities, charms and taken-for-granted abilities that people have. They can look back on a life that was lived and remembered for perhaps one single attribute.

I'll always remember Aunt Kitty's rolls, and I'm sure Ada Horton's family and friends who bought the rolls before they ever appeared on the food sale table, will never forget them.

Precious Moments

I attended a wedding recently in the Berkshires which was a lovely outdoor affair with no rain in sight. What a fair day for the newlyweds as the sun shone and the soft breezes of summer swept over the beautiful outdoor setting. This wedding was special to me because 35 years ago I held this bride — then an infant — as she was presented for baptism. That made her very special to me.

When I made preparations for my apparel I debated about wearing a long gown. I had such apparel, but decided at the last minute to go for something a little more reserved and wore a georgette waltz-length gown that I call my "wedding dress."

I call it this because I wear it only to weddings; I bought it for my elder son's wedding 15 years ago. When I tried it on it was a bit snug but I could wear it. Later I wished I had persisted and gone with the long gown as very lovely creations and ensembles were worn by the ladies at the wedding. I felt quite dated.

I hunted up the little shoulder bag to carry my crying handkerchief and spectacles in and was happily surprised to find two mementos of previous weddings that I attended. In a little side pocket there was a match folder with the date July 2, 1988. (With the smoking ban now match folders are no longer given.) The other memento was the ceremony folder of a grandniece who was married in Pennsylvania in 1990. Can you believe that one hangs on to possessions such as these for so many years? I guess I'm just a sentimentalist and sort of save things like this. They are truly remembrances of happy events.

Weddings nowadays take on variations, some traditional and some very unusual. This last wedding was such a lovely affair and my godchild was strikingly beautiful in her long gown. I thought about how I used to gaze at her, an infant, such a beautiful, bright-eyed little bundle. She has carried that loveliness with her through the years. Her pet name for me is "Tante."

My granddaughter was with us at this wedding. Her mother whispered quietly to me that they should probably be saving right now for her wedding. This was an elaborate wedding and I'm sure my granddaughter might be thinking about her big event — years from now, I hope.

I cry at weddings. People still cry at all kinds of events such as baptisms, graduations, movies, honors and funerals. They may be tears of sorrow or joy, but come they will when dear ones are involved.

Now that my trip to the wedding is over I tucked away in my memory bank the happy sights and sounds. There were no matches, no printed napkins, and bottles of bubbles instead of rice were distributed. Just memories of that lovely bride and the other members of the wedding. 'Twas a happy day for this now-old godmother.

Token Christmas

The dining room table which has been my wrapping center for gifts is now cleared of its clutter. The tags, ties, bows, rolls of paper, scotch tape and wrappings are all put away. I have finished my Christmas gift wrapping ahead of time.

What a glorious time it was for me. I insisted that my family observe a "token" gifting this year. Gifts under the tree in profusion is not my idea of how we should celebrate this significant holiday. It's so commercial. The children used to make lists of things they wanted — we did too in fact — as if giving and getting gifts was the most important part of this special day.

That was when they — and we — were young and the commercialism of the season dictated the wants. As one grows older there are fewer things needed or wanted. I feel the need to fasten on to the significance of Christmas.

But to go with the flow I have agreed to some gifts. My, won't my children be surprised when they open their packages from me on Christmas morning! They will find these prettily wrapped packages hold some of the lovely lovelies they have given me through the years. There will be a delicate china serving dish given to me by my older son 40 years ago when he was a student in college. He spent a tidy sum on this exquisite piece. It will just as lovingly be given back to him this year. Also there will be the tassel from his mortar board in another box.

My sons are much too old for scrapbooks I know, but there are things that must be passed on — or back. They need to know that I catalogued and saved these items through the years. I believe they will be gently and happily reminded of things past. There are clippings from several stages of their lives. Lots of family newspaper stories and pictures fill the pages.

One son will find in his scrapbook detailed reports of his years spent in France at the University of Strasbourg; he trekked around Europe as a youth. He will find the clasp for his Cub Scout "neckerchief" that has laid hidden in one of my bureau drawers. This son will also receive the miniature ceramic pitcher which he sent me from Europe. Years ago they served cream in those little individual containers. (They still may do it that way.) I have treasured them through the years and now it is time to give them back.

I don't want to appear cheap or chintzy but I am observing a "token" Christmas gifting. I hope it has more meaning for my sons than a new computer, a heavy woolen scarf, warm gloves or a sizable check.

From Scratch

Exhaustion! That is the feeling I had from baking a cake from scratch for a family birthday. I can't believe how much physical exertion went into that creation which incidentally didn't turn out any better than a Duncan Hines or other pre-mixed brand.

I got out my oldest cookbook and found a recipe for a burnt-sugar cake, remembering that years ago I had made a prize offering with that recipe. I assembled all the ingredients, oiled the cake pan dusting it with flour (as we used to do), softened the butter, had the eggs at room temperature and was ready to create.

Ahead of time I had purchased a box of cake flour (there were few boxes of any brand on the grocery shelves) and had read how to caramelize or burn the sugar. I was ready to begin. First the butter and sugar had to be creamed. It was a laborious task and wasn't going well so I got out my electric beater to finish the creaming. The caramelized sugar was waiting to be added to the batter. Sifting the cake flour was important to properly mix it with the baking powder and pinch of salt. Two egg yolks had to be beaten; that meant separating the whites from the yolks. That was another little side task that I was clumsy doing.

Following directions to this point I was ready to add the caramelized sugar. It had turned to a sticky mess. It hadn't done that before. So I put it back on the stove and reduced it to the proper liquid texture. The egg whites had to be beaten and folded into the batter. By that time my arm was tired, my brain was addled, and the mixture didn't look like it did years ago. Nevertheless I put it into the cake pan and stuck it in the oven with a prayer that it would turn out like I envisioned it.

Back in the old days when a housewife tested the doneness of a cake she would pull a broom straw out of the top of the broom and use that as her tester. If it came out clean the cake was done. Luckily I didn't have to find the broomstraw, I had a handy toothpick.

The cake was put on a cookie rack and I began to make another batch of burnt sugar for the frosting. I was doing this by guess and b'gosh, so often the way my mother did. It did turn out to be a fair frosting mixture.

Voila! My promised burnt-sugar birthday cake.

I warned my guests that when I put the burnt-sugar into the batter it didn't mix well and perhaps they might find some hard crystals. Somehow or other the burnt sugar was absorbed and became a part of the cake.

How our mothers used to do all these laborious tasks is beyond me. My arm was sore, I was actually perspiring after putting this cake together. And I even had to sit for a spell before I could get up and remove the cake from the oven.

Never again will I bake a cake from scratch. Incidentally, does anyone want a half box of Swansdown cake flour?

Free-wheelin'

A recent article in *Time* magazine stated that "Bikes are back." It showed pictures of older people riding bicycles and declared it is a gung-ho exercise for knees that can no longer take the shock of running and other exercises. The article also stated that more than seven million riders over 60 are riding two wheelers. This statistic according to the League of American Bicyclists.

I confess with embarrassment that I never learned to ride a bicycle. But I tried! When I was a youngster I got on the neighbor kid's bike and started to ride on a little downgrade on the sidewalks. Immediately I took a spill, got up, looked at my bruised elbows and sore knees and vowed I would not try it again. I didn't like to get hurt.

I don't recall my first son learning to ride a bicycle because he was visiting his grandparents and the neighbor kids had bikes. He was not afraid of falling off and taking a spill. The clamor to buy him a bike was soon heard. No problems for him. And when he went off to college he had a small Indian motorcycle to tool around the campus. That really frightened me as kids get sort of reckless and show-offy when they get away from home.

When my second son was ready to learn to bicycle he borrowed a neighbor kid's bike and the two of us went to the alley to begin the trials. I steadied him on that bike until he was pedaling along. Soon he tipped over and ended up with hurts and bruises. He got right up and started over. Before the lesson was over he had mastered the balance on a two wheeler. I was proud but a bit disgusted with myself that I hadn't persevered.

It made me very proud when this second son decided to take a youth hostel biking tour of Europe at age 17. His European bike was bought in London and served him well with its 15 speeds as he wheeled through Europe. That bike still stands in his garage, but he doesn't have time to bike. Perhaps when he gets to that stage when the knees need extra exercising he may shine up that 15-speeder and go tooling along like the rest of the oldsters do.

I see TV commercials with oldsters riding serenely along with a group and wish that I had persevered. They look so pleased doing this exercise, and those cute helmets indicate that they are serious about safety when they ride.

I do bike now, but that bike is not out in the open and I do not have to worry about it tipping over. You see, I'll have to be content with a stationary exerciser, because I was too much of a pantywaist years ago to take the spills and accomplish outdoor bicycling.

That's Really "Cracker Jack"

*A*s youngsters it wasn't often that we got a whole box of Cracker Jacks for ourselves. We shared, of course, and I always wanted the molasses-coated peanuts. It was a rule that we had to wait till we got to the bottom of the box before we could get the little prize. It wasn't much of a prize but the excitement of knowing there was one in the box was always there.

Cracker Jacks became a treat at the 1893 World's Fair in Chicago. It was concocted by a German immigrant and eventually became one of our first American "snack" foods. When F.W. Rueckheim saved $200 from farm wages in 1871 he opened a small popcorn stand in Chicago. He added peanuts, caramel, marshmallows and taffy to his line. He finally reasoned that if customers enjoyed all these treats he'd put them together in one combination. Thus began Cracker Jacks.

When it came time to chose a name for the confection, a friend exclaimed after eating it, "That's crackerjack!" and the name stayed. The first boxes didn't include a prize as it wasn't until 1912 that little toys were added. That's the year I was born; it not only marked my birth date but the year that Cracker Jacks gave its product that name.

I like this treat, and my husband would buy it in large boxes when we went to the movies. We didn't need the excitement of finding a prize in the big box in a darkened theatre.

Since 1912, when the prizes were added to the small boxes, more than 17 million toys have been made for the boxes. It is quite a hobby for collectors to acquire these little gems; there is now a Cracker Jack Collectors Association with a web site. I'll bet the prizes they put in the boxes nowadays are really weird looking things. I learned they are called "Nits" and have been appearing since the early 1970s.

I think I'll go buy a box of Cracker Jacks and see just what a "Nit" looks like. And I won't wait till I get to the bottom of the box to find my prize; I'll dump the contents into a dish and get all the peanuts and probably throw the "Nit" away. I'm not into collecting odd things these days.

Christmas Specialties

I was talking to a group of ladies the other day and they talked about their holiday specialty. One woman said she doesn't do crafts or make fancy things but she does like to make candy. These tasks take on meaning because they are done for others and are a seasonal activity.

My father liked to make candy at Christmas time. His specialty was peanut brittle. When it was ready to cool he took the low flat pans and set them in the snow to cool before cracking it into pieces. Another thing we did was to make taffy. Who knows what taffy is these days? If you've ever been to a boardwalk you know about salt water taffy, but did you ever see it made? When we made taffy, oh so many years ago, it was with old-fashioned sorghum. This product was made from a grain that has to be processed and boiled in huge kettles. It was then poured into gallon pails with bails on them. I watched a neighbor make such batches of this thick brown syrup on an open fire.

When we made taffy we boiled the sorghum to the right consistency; tested it by putting a drop in cold water. The mixture was then cooled; we buttered our fingers and began to pull the stringy mass. From a dark brown color it became a glistening whitish confection. The mixture was stretched into strands and then cut into "kisses." It was a sticky mess, but oh it was so good.

It used to be a social event to have a taffy pull. I can't imagine what that would be like today. Who would want to have that kind of a messy party particularly if it was a group of kids who were not familiar with taffy making.

One lady said she liked and made good fudge. Another's specialty was fondant and divinity. Those take a real talent to make.

And so the conversation went about specialties. I had to tell them that my holiday specialty is a steamed pudding. My mother used to make a pudding using suet. (Who knows what suet is today?)

Years ago I discovered a recipe for a steamed pudding which doesn't use suet; it calls for raw potatoes, carrots, currants, raisins, spices, flour and shortening. It is steamed for three hours, properly cooled and taken out of the mold. A tube mold is hard to find these days, but you can substitute a coffee can and cover it tightly with foil for the steaming process. It gives it a little pizzazz if made in the container that has a stem in it.

I received a request from my California son for two steamed puddings for his Christmas feasting. I hand delivered them to him in California for Christmas. Carrot pudding is my specialty.

Big City Honeymoon

I was treating my daughter-in-law to lunch one day in January and our conversation drifted to that particular date. It was 65 years ago that I was married and I was giving her a review of that event. She said it sounded like one of my articles aborning, so here it is:

That day in 1936 the thermometer must have been hovering around the zero mark. Guests were coming from out of town and were concerned about the road conditions. Our hour was set at 4:00 so guests could get started on their homeward trip before darkness fell. Therefore, we had no reception as is usual with a church wedding. This event took place in a little Kansas town called Morrill.

Our car had been hijacked by some fun-loving groomsmen and they left it stuck in a snowdrift at the edge of town. It took quite a time after the ceremony to find the car and allow us to leave on our honeymoon trip. It was to be a short one as we were married on Sunday and were due to take over our little country newspaper the following week.

I was explaining to my daughter-in-law Janice, that we had a "due bill." She was unfamiliar with that so I explained that it was a "freebie" two-night stay at the State Hotel in Kansas City. It had been acquired by my father for advertising the hotel in his Kansas weekly.

So off we went in the snowy darkness headed for Kansas City, which if I remember correctly, was 100 miles away. We were excited about being married, about taking over a business and planning our future. Little did we know what lay ahead of us in our venture.

When we arrived at the (old) State Hotel which was a respectable hostelry at the time we were given a nice room and planned our next two days. We had appointments with firms regarding the improvement of our little newspaper and one was with the manager of the Western Newspaper Union. (It is probably not in operation now by that name.) We planned to use a supplement which would give canned world-wide and national news, recipes and useful information to our rural reading public.

The WNU manager picked us up by taxi and we followed him into the huge Kansas City Athletic Club dining room. When he asked what we would have to drink I was puzzled. He insisted that we must have something to celebrate our wedding and suggested Manhattans. The first one tasted pretty swell and I was invited to have another. To someone who had no idea about "spirits" I was overly brave. Well! By that time we could have signed for just about any service the company offered.

After a fine lunch we went back to our hotel as I was feeling the effects of those two Manhattans. It was bitter cold and we cancelled our other appointments. Later we thought it would be grown-up to have dinner in our room. After ordering it we were surprised to hear a knock at our door and the bellboy delivered a magnum of champagne — a gift from the WNU manager who had just treated us to lunch.

Our dinner arrived and was set out in our room. What would we do with a magnum of champagne? What fools we were! We drank the whole magnum. If you know anything about champagne you know that you don't consume it in that amount. We didn't know! But consume it we did. I can't tell you the rest of the story because it somehow failed to register in my numbed brain and body.

The next day reality took over and we started to the little town in Kansas, woozy but wiser! We began to contemplate the big task ahead of us. I've written about our weekly newspaper adventures before so won't go into that. I will say that my introduction to spirits consumed in a huge and not particularly wise way taught me an early lesson. And thus I finished the story that Janice thought might be something you would read.

Wrinkle Parade

I don't want to bore you about my last year's family reunion in Kansas, but such an event for four remaining siblings is something that will linger in our tired old memories for a long time. I knew when we got together and I saw my sisters and brother that we would compare wrinkles!

Strange what nature does to us as we age. My brother's wrinkles were not visible because he has kept his weight (too much, of course) and there was no shrinking or puckering of his skin. The oldest of us (94) has stayed thin all her life and instead of having furrows or wrinkles her skin fell in soft dewlaps, or little pockets around her cheeks. She looked the best preserved of us all! She is the one who carried the cane and three days in a row she was game to drive the 70 miles from Nebraska to join us.

Recollections of my favorite Aunt Ethel who lived to be 94 brought to mind how she had such a beautiful skin in her old age. Whenever she visited us she had an array of unguents, astringents and creams which were no doubt part of her wrinkle control.

One wouldn't assume that we were a very handsome looking set of remaining siblings. But we were all alert and could reach back in our memories and come up with some of the darnedest happenings as we were growing up. We talked about how we wore hand-me-downs; clothes were usually handmade and with stronger materials. That is why they lasted so long and could be handed down two and sometimes three times. But that was part of the fun; joining in laughing at ourselves as we grew up in a quite different world than our children are living in. We all knew what it was to work hard. My sisters learned how to keep a neat house. That was never my forte and to this day I hate the thought of dusting.

We talked about how we slept three in a bed and how we hated those double flannel blankets that somehow came untucked as three tykes rolled around in their sleep. Present day household chores were compared to how difficult they were years and years ago. All of us sisters were widowed and bemoaned that fact. Fortunately all three of us have the advantage of living near children who willingly, kindly and gently look after us if need be. Our consensus was that we wouldn't change that facet of our lives and are grateful to have sons and daughters who care.

Wrinkles, hand-me-downs, three-in-a-bed, times with no expensive toys, a work ethic which has kept us busy all our long lives, laughs and a few tears earmarked this gathering which we could easily call the "Wrinkle Parade."

Chautaqua Week

One of the words in last year's national Spelling Bee was Chautauqua. Not only did I know how to spell it, but I remember how Chautauqua brought adult and youth programs to small towns. A long time ago this was a summer attraction and the highlight of the season. Chautauqua is a town in southwestern New York State where these summer education programs originated. I'm not sure that they still go out on a road show basis these days.

These summer programs originated back in 1874. On one of our trips through New York State we visited the Chautauqua Assembly grounds and saw how this summer program brings live cultural offerings to the area. One of my Massachusetts friends always took her vacation and went to Chautauqua for the summer events.

My recollection of Chautauqua goes back to my early days in Iowa. Each summer a large tent was erected in the city part or on the school grounds. A large stage was the focal point, and folding chairs were set up for the audience. Some very fine entertainments were presented at matinee and evening performances. There were musical groups, small combos, dramatic presentations, and even some scientific feats were performed. One that I recall showed how heat could be transmitted without a fire. That had to be the microwave we now have. At the time we thought it was hokum or magic, but how wrong we were.

Additionally there were morning activities for youngsters when we learned songs, played games and were given a preview of coming performances. We never missed those Chautauqua-for-Kids sessions.

The large tent held around three or four hundred people. The side flaps were rolled up so air could pass through because midwestern summers were hot. Funeral homes or banks provided paper fans; each folding chair had a fan on it.

This was the anticipated summer educational and cultural event. Chautauqua lasted one week with a different performance each day. The performers were on a circuit and went from small town to small town keeping the country folks up on the latest entertainments. Well-known or lesser actors made the scene and may have gone on to Broadway.

It is all a little vague to me now, but I learned to spell Chautauqua because it was a reality then. No wonder that young man missed the word in the spelling bee; they don't seem to do traveling Chautauquas these days.

Wash Day

A young child asked me what makes soap bubble. I told her that soap is composed of molecules with two different properties one rubbing beside the other that latches on and takes away the dirt and grease in a garment. Soap has always been made with fats. The Phoenicians in 600 BC concocted the first soap by blending goat fat with wood ash. The first successful clothes washing detergent named Tide appeared in 1946.

It brought back the time when I was a youngster and in our home every Monday morning was wash day. My first memory of our washing machine was one with a wooden tub and a lever mechanism that you pushed back and forth to agitate the clothes.

But first the water had to be heated in a big old copper boiler which was filled the night before. Clothes were sorted according to color and fabric. Then a bar of laundry soap was shaved into the boiler and the water poured into the old tub type washer.

We all took our turn at agitating that washer. There was a wringer attached to a wash tub which was set on a wash stand. After running the clothes through the ringer into the first water it was attached to a second tub and another rinse followed. In the second tub was a little bag of blueing balls that was to add whitener to the clothes. Later I recall blueing in a liquid form.

Then out to the clothes line which was a wire one stretched between poles, usually three or four lines. We learned to hang sheets just so, towels had to be pinned on the line with three clothespins. The clothespins were in a hanging bag, or you wore a clothespin apron. We never had snap clothespins; they were the old fashioned straight one-piece kind which people use now in crafts.

A bright sunny day always dried the clothes quicker and they were then gathered and brought inside to fold and sort. If they needed to be ironed they were sprinkled (usually by a dash of water with the hand) rolled and put into a basket ready for ironing the next morning.

What drudgery! But not as bad as when women bent over a washboard and scrubbed clothes by hand. In some countries women still wash clothes by pounding them on rocks by the river. Sailors at sea used to put their clothes in a bag and hang them over the side and let the ocean movements clean them.

How wonderful to have our modern gadgets that make wash day a breeze. You can put them in a machine, walk away and do a dozen little tasks before you have to attend to them. There is no more drying out of doors these days and that is a convenience too. But you don't get that fresh air smell that we always experienced oh so many years ago.

Paper Dolls

I saw an ad the other day about a new kind of paper doll. It had a sturdy wooden base and was dressed by "gluing" clothes on a sturdy felt-like image. It was listed as a learning tool rather than a play item.

Paper dolls were a great favorite of mine as a kid and we spent many hours dressing the paper favorites in their assorted outfits. *McCalls Magazine, Ladies Home Journal* and *Woman's Home Companion* always had a page of paper dolls. We were permitted to tear out that page and cut out the images. But we were not allowed to use my mother's dressmaking shears and had to cut with those blunt type school scissors.

My younger sister and I often visited an aunt and uncle in the country. One of our best play times was going up into the attic and going through all those accumulated magazines and finding that page of paper dolls. This farm house formerly belonged to a family who retired and moved to California, and my aunt and uncle were tenant farmers. This family saved everything in that attic. Perhaps they intended to reclaim all these stored goods, but for several years we had access to all those old magazines where we found our beloved paper dolls.

The problem with paper dolls in those days was that the little tabs that held the clothes on would break off long before we were tired of dressing the dolls.

This new paper doll is a durable toy, sort of like the old flannel board technique where you press something on and it stays. This type sounds more durable than our old timey cut-outs.

We kept our paper dolls in shoe boxes. Those days when you bought a pair of shoes they were always in a box, wrapped in tissue paper and the toes were always stuffed with something to help them keep their shape. Nowadays you often come out of the shoe store with a plastic bag for your purchase.

My sister and I would spend hours up in that attic so many years ago. I wish I could remember what happened to all our paper dolls. We brought them home and somehow they either lost favor or were thrown away. We knew there would be another issue coming out in the next month. Or perhaps we outgrew that pastime.

I think I would have enjoyed the kind of paper dolls that are put out now. They seem to have shoes, hair ribbons, wigs, etc., whereas our paper dolls just had dresses and hats.

Nice to know paper dolls are still around, but I've outgrown my desire for them!

Seeing Clearly

I was quite surprised the other day when a friend told me she saw my thank you article in a book at a doctor's office. It was included in remarks by people who had undergone eye surgery. I had quite forgotten I sent this note after eye surgery three years ago.

Even though it is an everyday occurrence for a surgeon to bring new sight to his patients with his skill, it is a big item to us seniors as we journey down our later years.

As we grow older our bodies need repairs and restorations. I was nearing the end of my eighth decade and discovered that my sight had dimmed. I couldn't see clearly those little green arrows on the stop lights.

I approached eye surgery with the usual fear. So many people who had gone through it said it was "a piece of cake." The surgeons and technicians who were to guide me through this experience were kind, skilled and compassionate.

My first operation was a question mark to me. The pre-admission and pre-op procedures were handled efficiently. I was calm with only a wee idea of what was to take place. Nevertheless I felt something magic was happening.

In a short while I was informed that the surgery was over. A recovery time followed, I was given my post-op orders and allowed to walk out of the clinic.

That was the first operation. A few weeks later I went back for the second procedure. The same care and professionalism followed. Except that I knew what to expect. After it was over I put on the solar shield glasses and walked into the bright sunlight of a late fall day. Arriving home I followed post-op orders. A bit tired I decided on an early bedtime. I fell asleep sure that by morning I would be back to normal, because medical skill had made this new sight possible. Jubilation!

I have joined the large army of people who have gone the cataract/lens implant route. Life has taken on a new depth. I see normally and read with my "drug store" glasses, see distances and other sights not clearly discerned before. Another of life's blessings for the elderly.

I may just go on and live another decade now that I have these "new eyes."

Writing Tools

A few days ago a friend sent me an article clipped from the *New York Times* with a picture of an old 1941 black Underwood typewriter, the prized possession of a former publisher and editor. Since I'm still a holdout as far as computers are concerned and use a manual typewriter, I thought you might enjoy this tale.

The writer talked about his typewriter "crashing." (I thought only computers did that!) But his ribbon stalled, the keys drilled holes where it stopped, the "n" hit above the line and the "a" and "q" jammed and the "s" wandered, so finally he abandoned the machine. He had had that Underwood for 37 years.

The man's children argued for a computer for him. They told him that instead of recopying "whole pages" he could simply edit the words on the screen. He didn't have to use carbon paper or make messy changes. They told him he would save time and that a computer would flag his grammar and correct his spelling.

This author loved his Underwood Standard typewriter. He liked the sound it made, the speed to which he had become accustomed to writing on it, and the way it echoed the rhythms of his thoughts. He even liked the pain it bred in his shoulders when he typed for too many hours. His heart, not the machine, made the eloquence of his writing; he wanted less speed not more, he stated.

In the end the author's son set up a computer for him and even arranged lessons. The night after the first lesson he had chest pains and nightmares. So at 3:15 he got up and looked at his old dead Underwood Standard wondering if he was short-sighted or long on sentimentality to miss it so much. The computer terrified him and he begged his son to remove it. He then haunted old business machine stores and found a Royal Standard with a soft roller and a touch as crisp as his old-fashioned Underwood Standard.

The author, Nick Lyons, former publisher of Lyons Press, says his typewriters (he bought several) have more human measure and that attracts him as so much of the past does because there's so little of it left. He says, a "part of him prefers not to rush or even keep up, but to keep at least a few fingers on older, simpler tools."

He ends his column by saying that every time he uses his standard typewriter that he "throws a few grains of sand into the bowels of the computer — and intends to keep doing so."

Aha! I have a kindred soul in that man. I'm happy as a clam with my old Brothers Compactronic 300, and a computer sits alone in my basement in the boxes it came in.

Proof We Can Bring 'Em Back

A recent issue of the *Bennington Banner* had an article and picture of MASS MoCA, the Museum of Contemporary Art in North Adams. It showed this huge art center which formerly housed the bustling Sprague Electric Co. That picture brought back many memories of that town just over the Vermont line in Massachusetts.

In 1958 — almost a half century ago — our little family moved from Alabama to North Adams. The late George A. Lerrigo became the administrator of the North Adams Hospital. We had moved to what looked like a decaying mill town with empty textile mills and turn of the century structures. It was in a state of urban renewal and the town fathers were aiming to recapture its former grandeur.

In due time urban renewal was completed. Streets were rerouted and a new attitude prevailed in North Adams. Sprague Electric was big-g-g and employed more than 4,000 people. The city prospered and a new wing was added to the hospital and dedicated to the late George Lerrigo who had served as its administrator for 20 years.

The story mentions the deterioration of housing after Sprague Electric closed down. There was one particular empty Victorian house on Church Street that we purchased "for a song" in 1960 and restored. It had lovely imported woods, four fireplaces with imported ceramics in their construction. Wide porches ran across the rear upper and lower stories, and at one time there was a porte cochère at the side entrance. It was built in 1890 in the horse and buggy days, with a stable in the rear. Those features were torn down before we purchased the house.

The long windows had inside shutters all in very good condition. The heavy iron weights for raising the windows were two feet in length. Old-fashioned chandeliers hung from molded ceilings in the main rooms. The house had four heavy sliding doors to close rooms off in winter and they rolled as smoothly as the day they were installed.

There were beautiful combinations of imported woods in the wainscoting in the downstairs rooms, with much hand tooling done on the framing of them. The long double front doors had Venetian glass inserts emblazoned with the letter "W" which was the initial of the Witherell family who built the house in the 1890s.

This Victorian house had a cupola (we called it a tower). It would have made a fine studio for a budding artist, but we never used the third floor. It must have been used for living quarters for the help as we noted there were gas jets still in place in these rooms. Whenever we had young visitors they always wanted to climb to the tower to look out over the town. 'Twas an interesting abode for 12 years of my life.

When I moved to Vermont I went back to look at the old house. It had become a combined home/office for the new owner. Later it was sold and became a nursing home. After that it became student housing for the state college students until it was abandoned. The last time I saw it, it was an empty run-down structure.

That visit brought tears to my eyes. There was peeling paint on the double front doors which had been painted a ghastly blue over the fine imported wood. The shrubs had grown almost to the second story, and where once the porte cochère stood, the porch steps were tumbling down and the wooden lattice needed repair. That lovely old "Victorian Lady" was shorn of her beauty. How sad!

I hope that with MASS MoCA pulling in visitors someone will begin restoration of those old houses. And that someone will see that particular house on Church Street. I loved every old-fashioned bit of it. If MASS MoCA can bring prosperity to North Adams it may also help to revitalize the community to the point of house restorations. And once again maybe that old Victorian Lady will be a family residence.

"Feathers" from Abroad

As I walked through my woods the other day I found a feather that had fallen from some bird's body during flight. It reminded me of a saying I heard back in the late 1940s. The war was over and we had moved to Excelsior Springs, Mo. It was often our pleasure to have foreign guests visit us. One was from mainland China; she had come to the United States to study and was on her way to New York City.

She stayed overnight with us before leaving from the Kansas City Union Station for the Big Apple. When she left she gave me a lovely lawn handkerchief with a dainty design in one corner. Her remark as she handed it to me was "If you go a thousand miles you bring a feather." That statement has stayed with me through the years. What a beautiful way to express her thanks. I never pursued this Chinese adage, but it made sense to me. Here was a young girl from a faraway land wanting to say thank you and her way of saying it was to give a small gift and use an ancient Chinese saying.

I recall other foreigners we knew through the years. A young Indonesian had come to visit. His English was good, but he held fast to some of his ingrained habits. I had made up the guest room bed as usual and bade him welcome. Imagine my surprise to find that he had made his bed the next morning. Or did he? I learned later that he had slept on the floor. Not because the bed was uncomfortable, but that was the way he slept in Indonesia.

Another guest came to stay just until he found a place to live. He was working in our town and we befriended him. He was like "the man who came to dinner," except that he did pay room and board. He lived with us for two years!

We hosted two English cousins who were school teachers. Their one wish was to travel to the United States when they retired. And they did. We were able to chauffeur them around to airports and enjoyed their gracious company. How I loved their charming Old World ways and their English accent. They lived in Windsor and could see the castle from their house. Sure enough when we visited later in England we saw the old castle as we looked from their little cottage window.

Then there was that lovely couple from Wales who spent a few days with us while they were on a Rotary exchange visit to the States. I loved their Welsh terms and their jolly good spirits. They are a couple who left a very old plate as a parting gift.

There always seemed to be interesting guests who came through our doors. We were always happy to put them up for a night or two. Our welcome mat was large and we had great joy in meeting newcomers.

Trees and People, So Much Alike

Right now the focus of our area is on our beautiful foliage. The spectacle and choice of colors is like nowhere else. At least we New Englanders like to think we offer the best leaf peeping anywhere in the world. Perhaps the golden aspens of Colorado come in second. The many tour buses that come to our area attest that we are the prime beauty spot of the fall.

Have you ever thought about how like trees we people are? Trees talk to each other as they rub their leaves together. Leaves like people dance to the flutter of life's motions. When it rains they shed tears like we humans. The soughing of the pines is like people talking.

I looked out the window at a tall stand of trees the other day – a fall day – and I saw tall trees conversing with one another as they moved back and forth as gentle zephyrs stirred them. They seemed to sway back and forth in a neighborly way. I noted berries on the coniferous trees; they have their own Christmas decorations. Each tree had some special characteristic just as we humans do. The bark, size and shape of limbs and leaves, and of course in this season each seems to offer their own special coloring.

As I looked at this tall stand of trees I realized how like people they are – or we are like trees. Some trees grow straight, sturdy and strong and reach to great heights. Others angle off on a crooked path and live a life that is not symmetrical and true. However, nature seems to send out other branches from them and they redeem themselves with strong plants. Ultimately they all reach for the heavens for nourishment and direction.

Now in our season of color we find the leaves on a course of their own. I watched out my window and saw one leaf flutter to the ground. Another followed suit and it looked sort of like a ballet. Soon they will all have done the same dance and lie fallen and dead on the ground. The final scene shows the trees as they have bowed to winter's coldness. It is not the end, however. They only slumber 'til another season awakens them and know it is time to take on another drama of beauty. They go through phases just like people as we advance through the various stages of life.

Trees are individuals too just like humans. They have their own shapes and designs and provide us with an artful study. When they begin to change color they do it differently – just like people live their lives differently. Some change color quicker than other meaning they mature faster – just like people. First a patch of one tree begins to take on color, then another gets the idea and follows suit. Soon the whole area is aflame with color and beauty. So too do humans catch the spirit of life and bring beauty to the world.

After the trees have shaken or given up their leaves they look neglected, but they stand proudly showing their skeletons. They have not lost life or dignity. They are only waiting for that next season of growth.

Leaves lie wasted in heaps. They rustle as you walk through them; then they become soggy with moisture and become compost for the best growing season. They have lived their lives and are no more except as they bring new life in a different manner.

Again: how like trees we humans are. We grow and use our energies in our lifetime. Sometimes we scatter our time and talents and they are wasted or fruitless. We live until it is our time to fall to earth.

Trees and people – we are alike.

Ashes in the Sunshine

The sun had just begun to peep through the overhanging clouds as I, with my stepdaughter Edith and stepson Harry and his wife Dottie, prepared to distribute the ashes of my late husband, Ed Leidich. The setting was a cemetery in a small Pennsylvania town.

In our 70s Ed and I felt it important to make our funeral arrangements to spare our families those tasks. This was a second marriage and two families were to be considered. So we came up with what we felt would be acceptable to both families.

At age 84, Ed suffered a stroke. We had Living Wills drawn up because we felt keenly about not sustaining life when there was no quality to it. When the second stroke came, Ed stoically accepted the consequences. He wanted no heroic methods to prolong a life that would place him in a nursing home and he would become a burden.

At one time Ed's condition seemed to improve. However, we were called very late one night to come immediately to the hospital as his condition was critical. Edith and I spent a night of anguish. We called Harry in Virginia and he concurred that his father would not want to be in a nursing home and that we should do "what Dad wanted done." Thus his Living Will was honored.

We held a memorial service with my son, Charles, an ordained minister and our local minister, officiating. It was not until six months later that we were able to complete Ed's last rites. The four of us met at the Pennsylvania cemetery where his first wife, who died at a young age, was buried.

The sun was just beginning to burn off the early morning fog as we drove into the cemetery. At the gravesite Harry read from Ed's grandfather's Lutheran prayer book; the passages had been annotated by Ed. Concluding with the King James version of The Lord's

Prayer, Harry scattered the ashes and they fell in the area of Ed's first wife's grave, then sifted toward what would be my gravesite some day.

Suddenly the sun was in full glory. It seemed like an omen. The shining sun represented to us the celebration of Ed's life. The brightness broke the sadness of our mission.

When my time comes to leave this earthly realm, my plans are all in place. My minister son will conduct a brief service and then my ashes will be carried to Pennsylvania where they will be scattered near Ed's gravesite.

I urge all oldsters who have not done this advance planning to go about doing it. It helps the grieving and sadness of a family not to be burdened and make heart-breaking decisions. We made our plans while we were competent and the Living Will is a wonderful way to die with dignity. I want my Living Will honored!

Wrap all these decisions up in a nice package and hand it to your children with a pretty ribbon and they will thank and bless you. They will be able to focus on fond memories of the loving care, nurturing and attributes of their parents. Too, the grieving will be easier as they know their parents did not fear death.

I hope the sun comes into full glory the day my ashes fall gently over that gravesite in a little Pennsylvania cemetery.

About the Author

The author is a true Midwesterner born in Iowa, later living in Nebraska, Kansas and Missouri before moving to Georgia and Alabama. Then came a move to Massachusetts with her husband, the late George A. Lerrigo. She lived in Delaware and New Hampshire with her second husband, Edwin Leidich until his death in 1993.

Two sons and her extended family add luster to her life. Her sons are Rev. Charles Lerrigo of Berkeley, California, and George E. Lerrigo, who is a French teacher at Mt. Anthony Union High School in Bennington.

She lives by herself in North Bennington, Vermont in a little house tucked away amid the pines and birches.

IMAGES FROM THE PAST

Publishing history in ways that help people see it for themselves

It's a Slower Waltz: Memorable Days from a Long Life by Harriette Lerrigo-Leidich is the first book to be published as a Beech Seal Press imprint.

Also in print are the following Images from the Past books:

The Quotable Calvin Coolidge: Sensible Words for a New Century by Peter Hannaford

The Real Woodrow Wilson: An Interview with Arthur S. Link, editor of the Wilson Papers by James Robert Carroll

America's Song: The Story of Yankee Doodle by Stuart Murray

Washington's Farewell to his Officers After Victory in the Revolution by Stuart Murray

The Honor of Command: General Burgoyne's Saratoga Campaign by Stuart Murray

The Essential George Washington: 200 Years of Observations on the Man, the Myth, the Patriot by Peter Hannaford

Letters to Vermont (Volumes I and II) From Her Civil War Soldier Correspondents to the Home Press, Donald Wickman, Editor/Compiler

Rudyard Kipling in Vermont: Birthplace of the Jungle Books by Stuart Murray

Norman Rockwell at Home in Vermont: The Arlington Years 1939-1956 by Stuart Murray

Remembering Grandma Moses by Beth Moses Hickok

Alligators Always Dress for Dinner: An Alphabet Book of Vintage Photographs by Linda Donigan and Michael Horwitz

White Fire by Stuart Murray

Available at your local bookstore or from Images from the Past, Inc.
For information call us at 802-442-3204
888-442-3204 for credit card orders
PO Box 137, Bennington, VT 05201 with check or money order.
When ordering, please add $4.00 shipping and handling
for the first book and $1 for each additional.
(Add 5% sales tax for shipments to Vermont.)

www.ImagesfromthePast.com